Original title:
Wintersong

Copyright © 2024 Swan Charm
All rights reserved.

Author: Sabrina Sarvik
ISBN HARDBACK: 978-9916-79-690-0
ISBN PAPERBACK: 978-9916-79-691-7
ISBN EBOOK: 978-9916-79-692-4

Beneath the Sound of Silence

In shadowed corners, whispers lie,
A gentle breath, the silence sighs.
Thoughts like currents start to flow,
Beneath the dark, where dreams bestow.

Lost in echoes, time drifts slow,
Moments blend, the stillness grows.
Each heartbeat soft, a muted chime,
In the depth of peace, we find our rhyme.

Minds awaken, secrets share,
In the hush, we lay both bare.
Hope's gentle touch, a fleeting spark,
Guiding hearts through endless dark.

Silence weaves its calming thread,
Through quiet moments, souls are led.
Finding beauty in what's unseen,
In the still, our thoughts convene.

Beneath the sound, a world composed,
Where silence speaks, and life is posed.
In every pause, a story's trace,
Beneath the sound, we find our space.

A Canvas of Icy Wonders

Crystal shards that shimmer bright,
Painting dreams in frosty light.
Nature's brush, a pure delight,
A canvas formed of purest white.

Mountains gleam with icy grace,
Every peak, a timeless face.
Whispers of the winter's song,
In this realm, we now belong.

Snowflakes dance on chilly breeze,
Filling silence with such ease.
Each flake tells a tale so bold,
Of winter's charm, both fierce and cold.

Beneath the sky, pale stars emerge,
In the night, the spirits surge.
A tapestry of frost is spun,
In the heart of winter's run.

As the dawn reveals the scene,
A world transformed, so pure, serene.
In every corner, wonders gleam,
A canvas born from nature's dream.

The Hidden Beauty in Cold

Frost clings to branches, a delicate lace,
Whispers of winter in a silent embrace.
Snowflakes dance softly, a swirling delight,
Beneath the pale moon, the world shimmers bright.

Crystals of ice, in sunlight they gleam,
A canvas of whiteness, a waking dream.
Each breath a cloud, in the frosty air,
Nature's own secret, a beauty so rare.

Crystalline Echoes of Solitude

Silence envelops, a blanket of peace,
Each flake that descends brings thoughts to release.
Branches stand still, holding secrets untold,
In the heart of the winter, the magic unfolds.

Footsteps are muffled, lost in the night,
Shadows twist softly, just out of sight.
The air is electric, a quiet so dense,
Crystalline echoes, a moment intense.

A Tale Woven in White

Blankets of snow drape the earth low,
A canvas untouched, where soft breezes blow.
Stories of winter, in whispers unfurl,
Capturing magic, in a shimmering whirl.

Pines stand like sentinels, guarding the past,
While time drifts along, it flows ever fast.
Crisp air wraps around like a gentle embrace,
A tale woven in white, a serene, timeless space.

Shivers in the Quiet

Under the starlight, the world holds its breath,
In the chill of the night, we find beauty in death.
Frosty winds whisper, secrets so deep,
As stillness awakens, the memories creep.

Each sparkle of snow tells a story it knows,
Of dreams yet to blossom, where time softly slows.
In the heart of the quiet, shivers ignite,
Embracing the magic, in the stillness of night.

Frozen Reflections

In the mirror of ice, we see,
Shadows of whispers caught in glee.
The world wrapped in a silvery pale,
Each breath a ghost in the winter's tale.

Trees stand still, draped in white,
Silent sentinels of the night.
Branches bow with a gentle sway,
Holding secrets of the frosty day.

Footprints etched in the frozen ground,
Stories of wanderers, lost and found.
Each step a memory, crisp and clear,
Of laughter echoing, drawing near.

Moonlight dances on the icy lake,
A shimmering canvas, the stillness wakes.
Stars keep watch in a velvet sky,
As dreams unfold in a soft sigh.

Time stands still in this frozen space,
A moment captured, a tender grace.
In these reflections, we find our way,
Through winter's heart, where memories stay.

The Elegy of the Frost

Whispers trace the air so cold,
Tales of love and loss retold.
In the chill, a haunting plea,
Embers fade, yet still they flee.

Each flake a tear from the twilight sky,
Falling softly, as dreamers sigh.
Beneath the frost, our hearts reside,
In the shadows where memories hide.

Candles flicker in the muffled night,
Guiding souls to the path of light.
Frosted windows, a silent gaze,
Holding echoes of brighter days.

Bells toll softly, a mournful song,
In the stillness, where we belong.
Time drifts like smoke on the breeze,
In this elegy, our hearts find ease.

Yet in the frost, new life will grow,
As spring whispers beneath the snow.
In every ending, beginnings start,
An eternal dance within the heart.

Winter's Soft Inheritance

Snowflakes fall in a gentle weave,
Covering earth, as we believe.
A blanket white, so pure, so deep,
Cradles the world in a quiet sleep.

Frosted fields stretch far and wide,
Nature's bounty, a whispered pride.
Each grain of ice, a story spun,
Of winter's grace, a race once run.

Children laugh, with cheeks aglow,
Building dreams where the cold winds blow.
In every corner, joy's embrace,
Carving pathways in frozen space.

Underneath the vast gray sky,
The breath of winter will softly sigh.
Carrying echoes of days gone by,
Inheriting gifts, as seasons fly.

Through icy breath, we find our song,
A melody of where we belong.
Winter's heart, both fierce and mild,
Leaves us weary, yet ever wild.

Glimmers in the Chill

In the hush of the frosty morn,
Glimmers awake, the day is born.
Silver threads weave through the trees,
Painting the world with a soft breeze.

The sun peeks shyly, a golden smile,
Warming the earth for a little while.
A sparkling coat on every branch,
Dancing light in a winter's trance.

Footsteps crunch on the carpeted ground,
Nature's music, a symphony found.
In the whisper of frost, life stirs,
As hope unfurls, despite the blurs.

Time spins softly, like snow on air,
Glimmers of beauty everywhere.
In the chill, our hearts ignite,
Finding warmth in the coldest night.

As twilight blankets the world in gray,
Stars begin their gentle play.
Glimmers of promise, twinkling bright,
Guide us through a serene night.

The Art of Stillness

In quiet corners, whispers fade,
Time rests softly, a gentle shade.
The world outside, a distant hum,
Within our hearts, the silence drums.

Breath held captive, thoughts in flight,
The dance of shadows turns to light.
In stillness found, our souls converse,
A sacred space, a universe.

With every pause, the chaos thins,
A symphony where peace begins.
In tranquil moments, we are whole,
The art of stillness calms the soul.

Memory's Ice

Frozen fragments, time's embrace,
Moments linger, lost in space.
A glimmer faint, a fleeting sigh,
In memory's ice, we learn to fly.

Each crystal shard holds echoes clear,
Of laughter shared and whispered fears.
Time's gentle hand, a sculptor's art,
Shapes our past, yet tugs the heart.

With every thaw, we face the past,
What once was bright, now shadows cast.
In memory's ice, we brave the cold,
Stories woven, silently told.

Unbroken Silence

In the void where voices cease,
A quiet strength brings sweet release.
Thoughts like echoes, softly fall,
In unbroken silence, we hear it all.

The gentle hush, a powerful friend,
Where restless minds are free to mend.
Words unspoken carry weight,
In stillness speaks the heart's true fate.

Cradled in this sacred space,
A chance to breathe, to find our place.
From silence blooms a bright new dawn,
In unbroken silence, we carry on.

Trace of the Snowfall

Whispers of winter kiss the ground,
Each flake a story, softly bound.
In silken layers, secrets keep,
The trace of snowfall, a promise deep.

Blankets white in muted light,
Transform the world, enchant the night.
Footsteps lost in frosty air,
In every drift, magic's flare.

Beneath the sky, so vast and wide,
Nature's canvas, pure and tried.
From every flurry, dreams will grow,
The trace of snowfall, a gentle glow.

Frostbitten Leaves of Autumn Past

In whispers soft, the branches weep,
The colors fade, as old dreams sleep.
Crisp air carries memories near,
Of laughter lost, of yesteryear.

Amber hues in twilight's glow,
Dance like flames in winds that blow.
Each leaf a tale, of time gone by,
Underneath an open sky.

Golden moments, now but dust,
Entwined with nature's fragile trust.
In the stillness, echoes call,
Rustling softly, through it all.

An autumn's heart, so wild, yet tame,
Whispers of a distant name.
Frostbitten dreams, now cold and gray,
Yet beauty lingers, come what may.

As seasons turn and shadows blend,
In vibrant hues, we find the end.
With every gust that shakes the trees,
We hold the past, like falling leaves.

A Glimpse Beyond the Freeze

Beyond the frost, a hidden light,
A promise kept, in winter's night.
Each frozen breath, a secret shared,
In crystal silence, hearts are bared.

A flicker bright, beneath the snow,
Hints of warmth that softly flow.
With every step, in shadows bold,
We seek the tales that time has told.

The world stands still, a canvas wide,
Where dreams in slumber softly bide.
Yet in the quiet, hope is sown,
For spring to rise, with seeds we've grown.

The chill of night, a fleeting phase,
Outlined by stars, in winter's haze.
A glimpse beyond, where futures gleam,
Awake the heart, revive the dream.

With every breath, new sights we chase,
In frozen realms, we find our place.
So let the ice, in splendor freeze,
For life awaits, beyond the freeze.

Chasing Shadows in the Snow

In whispers soft, the shadows play,
As winter's breath sings night to day.
Each step we take, the snow will sigh,
A fleeting dance, as moments fly.

Beneath the moon's ethereal glow,
We chase the dreams that drift like snow.
With every flake, a memory spun,
In twilight's grasp, two souls as one.

Frosted paths, with secrets deep,
In silence, where our stories sleep.
Weaving through the chilled twilight,
Holding shadows, chasing light.

A world transformed, in muffled sound,
With every step, our hearts unbound.
In fleeting moments, laughter born,
Chasing shadows, before the morn.

In snow's embrace, our wishes flow,
Carved in dreams that gently grow.
Together bound, through night we roam,
In winter's heart, we find our home.

Lanterns in the Winter Night

Lanterns glow in the frosty air,
Whispers of warmth, in winter's stare.
Each flicker tells a tale of old,
In gathered warmth, our hearts unfold.

The night is hushed, a veil of peace,
In glowing orbs, the worries cease.
Beneath the night, the shadows dance,
In every light, a second chance.

Snowflakes swirl in the gentle breeze,
Wrapped in dreams of ancient trees.
The lanterns glow, a guiding star,
Illuminating who we are.

With every step, we trace the light,
Through winter's grasp, into the night.
The world asleep, yet spirits rise,
In radiant hues beneath the skies.

As whispers echo, soft and bright,
We find our way in the winter night.
In warming glow, we stand as one,
Together shone, until the dawn.

Nightfall's Serene Lullaby

As shadows whisper soft and low,
The twilight dances, breathes and flows.
A gentle hush blankets the night,
Where dreams awaken, taking flight.

The moonlight weaves through branches bare,
Casting silver on the cool air.
Each star a wink in deepening skies,
A tranquil peace, the heart complies.

Crickets sing their evening song,
In harmony, where they belong.
The world turns quiet, calm and still,
Wrapped in night, a soothing thrill.

The soft embrace of dusk's caress,
Brings forth thoughts we long to confess.
With every pulse, the night unfolds,
A tale of love only night holds.

In this serene and gentle gloom,
Whispers of dreams begin to bloom.
So close your eyes, let worries fade,
Embrace the peace that night has made.

Echoes of a Frigid Dawn

The icy breath of morning calls,
Through frozen fields and frosted spalls.
A hush surrounds, the world asleep,
While shadows dance on mountains steep.

Soft whispers brush the silent ground,
Where frostbitten dreams are spellbound.
The dawn breaks slowly, colors clash,
In vibrant hues, the dark turns ash.

Each crystal flake catches the light,
Reflecting hope in chilling night.
The air is crisp, a fleeting kiss,
As nature awakens, full of bliss.

Amidst the chill, life stirs awake,
In every breath, the heart will quake.
A world reborn, as warmth draws near,
Echoes of dawn, fresh and clear.

In shimmering light, the day ascends,
With every moment, winter bends.
Embrace the cold, the beauty found,
In echoes of a frigid dawn.

Glacial Serenade

Through icy crevices, still and deep,
The glaciers sing, while mountains weep.
A symphony of ice and stone,
In frozen realms, where winds have blown.

The creaks and groans of ancient might,
Resound beneath the pale moonlight.
Each note a story carved in time,
A tale of beauty, pure and prime.

In frigid air, the echoes soar,
A haunting hymn from nature's core.
The world is quiet, yet so alive,
In this glacial realm, dreams thrive.

Waterfalls freeze in shimmering grace,
Reflection caught in nature's face.
Each droplet glistens with delight,
A serenade of sheer pure white.

So listen close, let the heart sway,
To the glacial song of the day.
For in this cold, life finds its way,
In frozen echoes, we shall play.

The Stillness Beneath the Stars

In the cool embrace of twilight's grace,
Stillness reigns, a sacred space.
Stars awaken, twinkle bright,
Guiding souls through the night.

The world holds breath, in peace it lies,
Beneath the vast, infinite skies.
A tranquil hush, as shadows creep,
Into a dream, the heart shall leap.

Cradled in night's gentle arms,
Nature whispers, with all its charms.
Each star a beacon, glowing strong,
Leading the lost, where they belong.

As silence deepens, thoughts unwind,
In the stillness, solace we find.
United under the starry dome,
In night's pure heart, we are at home.

So let the world fade away, abide,
In the stillness, let dreams collide.
For beneath the stars, infinite and bright,
We find our truth in the quiet night.

The Flicker of Hearthside Stories

In the glow of candlelight, we sit,
Whispers dance like flames in the dark.
Tales of love, loss, and every bit,
Crafting memories that leave a mark.

Grandma's laughter, a melodic sound,
As we gather, wrapped in a quilt.
Hearts entwined, this joy we've found,
In every story, dreams are built.

Old photographs line the walls,
Faces smiling through time's embrace.
Echoes of history as night falls,
Each story finds its rightful place.

Moments captured in the flicker,
As shadows waltz across the floor.
With each heartbeat, our bonds grow thicker,
In the hearth, we are evermore.

When the fire dims and silence reigns,
We hold these tales close to our heart.
Hearthside stories, like gentle rains,
From our lives, they shall never part.

Tranquil Moments in the Stillness

The morning sun peeks through the trees,
   Birds serenade in soft, sweet tones.
   A gentle breeze, the leaves at ease,
  Nature whispers in hushed groans.

With each step on the dew-kissed grass,
    I find a peace in every breath.
Moments linger, allowing time to pass,
  In stillness, there's life, even in death.

    Clouds float by, a slow parade,
     Painting pictures in the sky.
     In this haven, worries fade,
   As time dances, we learn to fly.

  Beneath a bough, I close my eyes,
    Listening to the world unwind.
  Among the whispers, tranquility lies,
     In every sigh, solace I find.

As day turns to dusk and shadows blend,
   I cradle moments etched in gold.
   Within the silence, I can mend,
  A heart that's weary, a story told.

Cadence of the Sleet

The windows rattle as winds partake,
Sleet falls softly onto the ground.
A rhythm building, a song it makes,
Nature's music is all around.

Each drip and drop a fleeting sound,
A dance of ice in the chilly air.
In this symphony, magic is found,
With every note, I lose my care.

Footsteps crunch on a frozen ground,
Echoes fading into the night.
Moments spent, where stillness is crowned,
Wrapped in the warmth, embracing light.

Tall trees shiver, dressed in white,
Branches heavy with winter's beauty.
In this moment, everything feels right,
The world pauses, lost in its duty.

As stars emerge, the sky no longer gray,
The cadence of sleet begins to cease.
In the quiet, I find my way,
To hold the magic, to claim my peace.

Serenity Under a Blanket of Snow

A frosted world, all hushed and still,
Snowflakes dance in a gentle spin.
Nature's canvas, a masterful thrill,
Whispers of winter, our journey begins.

Blankets of white cover the trees,
Each step muffled, like time stands still.
In this haven, my heart finds ease,
Wrapped in silence, a beautiful chill.

The laughter of children fills the air,
As they sled down hills with glee.
Moments like these, so precious and rare,
In the snowy embrace, we are free.

Evening descends, the stars appear,
Illuminating the tranquil night.
Wrapped in warmth, I hold you near,
Under the blanket, everything feels right.

Serenity reigns, the world serene,
In the quietude, hope springs anew.
Under this blanket, we've both been seen,
Together in stillness, forever true.

Frostbitten Ballad

In the chill of night, shadows creep,
Winds whisper tales, secrets they keep.
Stars above shimmer, pale and bright,
A frozen world draped in white.

Footsteps crunch on snow so deep,
Echoes linger, memories seep.
Moonlight dances on icy streams,
Frostbitten visions haunt my dreams.

The trees stand still, their branches bare,
Silent watchers, they seem to care.
A haunting call in the frosty air,
Nature's breath, a sweet despair.

Through the dark, a soft light glows,
Fire's warm embrace, when the cold wind blows.
Gathered close, the stories unfold,
Of winter nights and hearts made bold.

With every breath, a mist appears,
Woven into the fabric of fears.
Yet in this cold, there's warmth to find,
In frostbitten tales that bind the mind.

The Song of Glistening Pines

Whispers of needles in the breeze,
Pines stand tall, with graceful ease.
Draped in silver, cloaked in snow,
Their quiet beauty gently glows.

Underneath the layers of white,
Life awakens, hidden from sight.
Branches sway with secrets untold,
Nature's stories in silence unfold.

A song of glistening, soft and bright,
Through frozen realms, it takes flight.
Melodies dance on the crisp, cool air,
Echoing dreams, both light and rare.

Footsteps trace paths in the snowy veil,
Following whispers on the winding trail.
Glistening pines, guardians of time,
Their watchful presence, pure and sublime.

In the hush of dusk, shadows play,
Nature's chorus, night turns to day.
Among the pines, our spirits soar,
In a world filled with wonder, forevermore.

Murmurs Beneath the Snow

Beneath the blanket, silence sleeps,
In winter's arms, a secret keeps.
Winter's breath, a soft embrace,
Tales of life in quiet grace.

Soft whispers rise from hidden ground,
Echoes of life, where hope is found.
Roots entwined in a frozen dance,
Nature's rhythm, a timeless trance.

Frozen branches sway and creak,
Murmurs of life, they softly speak.
Beneath the snow, the world holds tight,
Awaiting spring's warm, gentle light.

In the cold, stillness is king,
Yet within, the stirrings of spring.
Each flake a promise in the air,
Murmurs grow, a future to share.

As seasons shift, the ice will melt,
In every crystal, love is felt.
Beneath the snow, life waits to show,
The vibrant blooms of a new tomorrow.

A Canvas of Stillness

A canvas white, spread wide and free,
Winter's art, a sight to see.
Brushed with frost, it sparkles bright,
A scene of calm in soft twilight.

Footprints traced on the crystal sheet,
Stories captured, time can't defeat.
Each step forward, a fragile mark,
In a world that glistens, bright and stark.

Trees like sentinels stand in line,
Guardians of secrets, ancient, divine.
In their stillness, wisdom flows,
As nature whispers, the soft wind blows.

In moments hushed, the magic blooms,
Beneath the stars, the night consumes.
A canvas vast, where dreams collide,
In winter's grasp, our hearts abide.

With every glance, the beauty lifts,
Nature's glory, the greatest gift.
In stillness lies a world to seek,
An endless echo, soothing and meek.

The Chill of Distant Songs

In twilight's grasp, whispers roam,
The air is thick with forgotten tones.
Notes linger like ghosts in the mist,
Carried by winds that cannot resist.

Under the stars, shadows entwine,
Echoes of laughter, a world so divine.
Each chord a memory, soft and clear,
A symphony woven from dreams we hear.

The chill of night wraps us tight,
As melodies dance in silvery light.
Time fades quietly, lost in throngs,
Bound by the threads of distant songs.

A Haven in the Cold

Within the forest, still and deep,
Where frozen secrets gently sleep.
A cabin glows with welcoming cheer,
It stands as a beacon, drawing us near.

The hearth inside murmurs a tune,
Embraced by warmth beneath the moon.
Outside, the chill bites through the trees,
But here, heartbeats flow with ease.

Snowflakes drift, a soft ballet,
Painting silence in shades of gray.
With every breath, the world stands still,
A haven crafted, eternal thrill.

Starlit Frost

Beneath the dome of winter's night,
A tapestry of stars gleams bright.
Each twinkle sings of distant lands,
Where dreams are spun by icy hands.

The frost adorns the sleeping earth,
A delicate dance of quiet mirth.
Crystals shimmer, a jewel's embrace,
In nature's clutch, a tender grace.

With every step, a crunch in tow,
The chill bites sharply, soft and slow.
Yet in the dark, there's magic cast,
In starlit frost, where shadows last.

Lament of the Winter Moon

Oh moon so pale, in night you weep,
A silver tear for the frost to keep.
Beneath your gaze, the world is cold,
A tale of longing quietly told.

Your light cascades on barren trees,
Whispers of sorrow carried by the breeze.
The silence clings like heavy air,
In every heart, a tender care.

Through frosted windows, warmth is sought,
Yet longing lingers, a heavy thought.
In the stillness, shadows loom,
Echoing the lament of the winter moon.

Frosted Echoes

Whispers of winter's breath,
Dance through the frozen air,
Silent tales of ancient woods,
Wrapped in a frosty glare.

Brittle leaves beneath my feet,
Crackling like hidden dreams,
Each step a note of winter's song,
Echoes in silver streams.

The sun peeks through icy clouds,
Casting shadows long and pale,
In this world, so quiet and still,
Frosted memories unveil.

Branches draped in crystalline lace,
Glisten like stars at night,
Nature's art in purest form,
A breathtaking, frozen sight.

As twilight falls, the hues ignite,
A canvas of indigo and gold,
Frosted echoes linger on,
In stories yet untold.

The Silent Embrace of Snow

Snowflakes whisper to the ground,
In gentle, soft descent,
A world transformed in hush of white,
A peaceful, calm lament.

They cloak the earth in quiet grace,
Embracing every stone,
A silent wonder, pure and deep,
In winter's chill alone.

Footprints vanish in the depth,
Of this silken, snowy sheet,
Every trace of life, concealed,
Nature's secret, lost retreat.

The trees adorned in frosted dreams,
Stand silent, tall, and bright,
A symphony of icy tones,
In the stillness of the night.

As dawn awakens, colors blaze,
Against the sparkling glow,
In this brief, ephemeral grace,
The silent embrace of snow.

Beneath the Icy Veil

Beneath the icy veil of night,
Whispers linger, soft and light,
Secrets hidden from the sun,
Beneath the frost, dreams gently spun.

Shadows dance on silvered ground,
In the hush, a magic found,
Each breath a wisp of crystal air,
In this realm, beyond compare.

Frosted leaves, a treasure bright,
Glistening with morning's light,
Nature's symphony unfolds,
Beneath the veil, a story told.

Crickets chirp their winter song,
While frost-kissed branches sway along,
In the quiet, life persists,
Beneath the veil, a world exists.

As stars fade with the rising day,
The icy veil begins to fray,
Yet in the morning, while it stays,
Magic lingers, softly plays.

Frost-kissed Memories

Frost-kissed memories linger still,
Echoes of laughter, the winter thrill,
In the heart of quiet woods,
Where time flows soft as it should.

Icicles hang like crystal dreams,
Draped on branches, in sunlight beams,
Every glint a tale to share,
Frost-kissed moments, beyond compare.

Shimmering paths of sparkling white,
Guide me through the gentle night,
Where shadows blend with soft moon's glow,
In a world where memories flow.

Each breath a cloud, so crisp, so clear,
Frost-kissed memories drawing near,
In this season's soft embrace,
I find comfort in time and space.

As the season slowly fades,
And winter's chill starts to jade,
These memories in my heart remain,
Frost-kissed echoes of joy and pain.

Longing in the Cold

In the barren fields of white,
My heart wanders through the night.
Whispers echo in the breeze,
Longing for warmth, my soul's unease.

Frosted branches arch and bend,
Memories of love they send.
Silhouettes of dreams long past,
In the shadows, warmth will last.

The chill wraps me in its embrace,
Yet I seek your tender grace.
Each flake that falls from the sky,
Brings your laughter, drifting by.

Silent stars twinkle above,
But they can't replace your love.
Endless winter, time stands still,
I ache for you, my heart's own thrill.

As the dawn begins to break,
Hope ignites with each heart's ache.
Longing stirs the quiet air,
A promise waits, my love is there.

The Lure of the Winter Twilight

In twilight's grip, the world turns grey,
As shadows stretch, they softly sway.
The sun descends, a fading glow,
In winter's hush, the night will grow.

Chilling whispers, tales unfold,
Enchanting secrets, dark and bold.
The stars awaken, one by one,
A dance of frost beneath the sun.

Amidst the trees, the silence sings,
Of hidden dreams and silver wings.
A fleeting moment, time stands still,
Captured heartbeats, against the chill.

The moonlight drapes the world with care,
As winter dreams fill the cool air.
Each breath a cloud, a fleeting sigh,
In twilight's embrace, we learn to fly.

For in this hour, all hearts unite,
Drawn to the charm of winter's night.
The lure of dusk, a sweet refrain,
In every heart, we feel the pain.

Beneath the Silver Moonlight

Beneath the silver moonlight's glow,
The world transformed, a shimmering show.
Each step a whisper on the snow,
A silent path where wishes flow.

Shadows dance in the gentle breeze,
Crystalline leaves upon the trees.
I wander lost in dreams so bright,
Guided by stars, through the night.

The cold wraps tightly, a tender veil,
Stories drifting like a fragile sail.
As time slips past like melting ice,
In this haven, I feel divine spice.

Silent echoes of laughter ring,
With every heartbeat, the night takes wing.
Lost in reverie, the heart takes flight,
Embracing love beneath moonlight.

In this moment, all feels right,
Bathed in the warmth of the night's light.
With moonlit dreams, my heart shall soar,
Beneath the stars, forevermore.

Harmony of the Icy Night

In the stillness of the icy air,
A symphony plays, without a care.
Crystals glisten in the pale light,
Harmony found in the freeze of night.

The world is hushed, wrapped in white,
Softly glowing, a peaceful sight.
Every snowflake, unique in design,
A fleeting note in a world divine.

Winds gently weave through branches bare,
As echoes of winter fill the air.
In twilight's embrace, the magic grows,
A harmony born where love bestows.

Each heartbeat resonates with the chill,
As dreams arise on the frosty hill.
Together we stand in pure delight,
A sweet serenade of the icy night.

Let's dance through the shadows, hand in hand,
In this frozen wonderland we'll stand.
For in this harmony, love ignites,
Forth shining bright through these wintry nights.

Winter's Soliloquy

Whispers of snow upon the ground,
A silent world without a sound.
Branches bare against the sky,
As frosty winds begin to sigh.

Each flake a story, soft and light,
Dances in the pale moonlight.
Crisp air wraps around like a shawl,
Echoes of winter's quiet call.

Footsteps crunching, a moment shared,
In the stillness, hearts are bared.
Nature resting, taking pause,
In hibernation's gentle cause.

Stars twinkle in the deep, dark night,
A world adorned in silver light.
With every breath, we feel the chill,
In winter's grasp, time stands still.

As dawn approaches, shadows fade,
Ice's grip beginning to wade.
Softly warming, the sun will rise,
Promising spring under the skies.

The Freeze of Time

In the stillness, moments freeze,
Time suspended, like a breeze.
Snowflakes twirl, a soft ballet,
In the quiet of the day.

Frosted windows, breath on glass,
Time drifts slowly, moments pass.
Every heartbeat, a whispered truth,
Echoes of forgotten youth.

Nature slumbers, dreams of white,
Wrapped in blankets, soft and tight.
Stars above in silent glee,
Watch the world in reverie.

Each second holds a breathless glow,
In winter's grasp, we come to know.
Every second savored slow,
As time stands still, our spirits grow.

The sun dips low, shadows extend,
Embracing winter, we descend.
In the silence, we find a rhyme,
A rhythm born of the freeze of time.

Beneath the Frosted Sky

Beneath the frost that softly lays,
The earth sleeps on in peaceful ways.
Wrapped in blankets, white and pure,
Nature waits, so calm, so sure.

Each breath released becomes a mist,
In winter's arms, we find our bliss.
Whispers float through icy air,
Promises linger, sweet and rare.

Footprints trace a fleeting dance,
In beauty found by happenstance.
The quiet speaks in hushed delight,
As day dissolves into the night.

Silver stars begin to shine,
In darkness, we see the divine.
A world transformed under the sky,
Where hopes and dreams can softly sigh.

Beneath the frost, the heartbeats thrum,
In winter's hush, together we come.
Amidst the cold, we find the warm,
In nature's cradle, we seek the charm.

Twilight's Gentle Grip

Twilight whispers, a soft embrace,
Nightfall dances, in its grace.
Colors fade, a gentle blend,
As the day begins to end.

Horizon blushes, a fleeting glow,
The stars awaken, one by one they show.
In the quiet, shadows grow,
A tapestry of twilight's flow.

Each moment held in tender light,
As day surrenders to the night.
Warmth of dusk upon the skin,
A peaceful sigh, where dreams begin.

Chasing fireflies in the dark,
Nature's whispers, a quiet spark.
Time suspends in twilight's grace,
In this stillness, we find our place.

Embrace the hues as day retreats,
In twilight's grip, our heartbeats meet.
With every breath, we feel the shift,
In the charm of night's sweet gift.

Frosted Starlight

In the hush of the night,
Stars twinkle so bright,
Each one a tiny flame,
Whispers calling your name.

Snow blankets the ground,
Silent magic is found,
Glistening diamonds fall,
Covering all, after all.

Moonlight bathes the trees,
In the chilled winter breeze,
Glowing in silver hues,
Painting the world anew.

Footprints left in the snow,
Tell stories that we know,
Of warmth in the cold air,
Moments cherished with care.

Dreams drift like the flakes,
In the peace that it makes,
Frosted starlight above,
Whispers of winter love.

The Dance of the Snowflakes

Snowflakes twirl and spin,
In a soft, gentle grin,
Each one unique and bright,
Dancing in the pale light.

They glide on frosty air,
Floating without a care,
Whirls of white in a flight,
Creating pure delight.

On rooftops, they gather,
In silence, they patter,
A carpet of pure white,
Transforming day to night.

Children laugh and play,
In this winter ballet,
With arms open wide,
Welcoming the soft slide.

The world wrapped in frost,
In this moment, not lost,
Nature's gentle embrace,
A magical, peaceful space.

Solitary Pines

In the forest so deep,
Where the shadows creep,
Pines stand tall and proud,
Silent in the crowd.

Their branches stretch wide,
Holding secrets inside,
Guardians of the night,
Bathed in silver light.

Whispers in the breeze,
Echo through the trees,
Each rustle a song,
Where the heart feels strong.

Snow rests on their boughs,
Nature takes her vows,
To keep the world still,
In the winter's chill.

Alone, yet not lonely,
Their presence, a phony,
Companions they keep,
In the silence, they seep.

Winter's Veiled Whimsy

With magic in the air,
The world transforms with care,
A blanket pure and white,
Cloaks the earth in night.

Glistening on the trees,
Dancing in the breeze,
Sparkles twirl and spin,
As the night wears thin.

Frosted breath in the cold,
Stories waiting to be told,
Nature's playful art,
Whispering from the heart.

As shadows take their flight,
Twinkling stars shine bright,
Each moment, a surprise,
Under winter's wise skies.

In this world of dreams,
Life is not as it seems,
Winter's whimsy calls,
As the magic enthralls.

Muffled Steps in a Snowfall

Softly fall the snowflakes,
Whispers in the night.
Footsteps hush beneath them,
In pure, enchanting white.

Silent paths are winding,
Moonlight's gentle kiss.
Every step a secret,
In the winter's bliss.

Branches bow with weight now,
Crystals all around.
Echoes of our laughter,
In this snowy ground.

Time stands still, forgotten,
Wrapped in frosty air.
Nature holds its breath,
In a world so rare.

Muffled steps, we wander,
Hearts in quiet tune.
Underneath the starlight,
Dancing with the moon.

Dreaming in a Frozen Palette

Brushstrokes of the twilight,
Cold hues intertwine.
Silhouettes of daydreams,
In frosted, silver lines.

Echoes of the twilight,
Breathe in chilly air.
Shadows softly shifting,
In winter's gentle care.

Canvas of the night sky,
Starry dots and gleams.
Painting dreams in silence,
As the world redeems.

Colors softly swirling,
Crimson, blue and white.
In this frozen palette,
We embrace the night.

Brush away the worries,
Find solace in the freeze.
In this art of dreaming,
My heart is at ease.

The Nightingale's Frosted Tune

Nightingale is singing,
Notes like crystal air.
Frosted trees are dancing,
With melodies to share.

Voices travel softly,
Through the snowy pines.
Chilling winds do carry,
Rhythms so divine.

Underneath the starlight,
Nature's sweet embrace.
Frosted tunes are weaving,
In this tranquil space.

Every note a heartbeat,
In the wintry night.
Nightingale, keep singing,
Your song is pure delight.

So let the frost hold gently,
While the world stands still.
In the nightingale's tune,
Hear the winter's thrill.

Veil of Flurries

Veil of flurries dancing,
Soft on whispered breeze.
Layer after layer,
Bringing hearts to ease.

Twinkling through the twilight,
Snowflakes kiss the ground.
Each one tells a story,
In their silent sound.

Nature wraps in white cloth,
Soft embrace of chill.
Every flake a moment,
Frozen dreams fulfill.

Glistening in shadows,
Fleeting, pure delight.
In the veil of flurries,
We find peace tonight.

A canvas draped in stillness,
Underneath the glow.
Veil of flurries falling,
In this world of snow.

Solstice Reverie

At dusk the sun begins to bow,
The stars awake, a silent vow.
Whispers dance on winter's breath,
In this hush, we find our depth.

Shadows stretch across the ground,
As ancient trees rise all around.
Fires flicker, warmth takes flight,
A gentle dream, the longest night.

Candles glow like tiny moons,
Caroling at night's soft tunes.
Heartbeats echo in the dark,
Glimmers of an inner spark.

Snowflakes twirl in blissful play,
Marking time till breaking day.
The world feels small, yet oh so vast,
Moments held, forever cast.

In the chill, we find our way,
Through the quiet of this stay.
With every breath a promise made,
In solstice peace, our fears will fade.

A Thrum Beneath the Drifts

Underneath the snowy veil,
Life's whispers start to prevail.
Roots entwined in silence deep,
Awake, the dreams that winter keep.

The earth beneath begins to hum,
Nature's pulse, a steady drum.
Frosted leaves, a silent choir,
In this stillness, we aspire.

Gentle winds weave through the trees,
Carrying secrets on the breeze.
Life persists in frozen realms,
Hidden strength within it dwells.

Each flake that falls, a tale unfolds,
In crisp air, the warmth it holds.
Paused moments, soft and bright,
Cradling dawn's first gentle light.

Lean in close, feel the thrum,
In winter's heart, life will come.
Through the drifts, a steady beat,
A promise held, and bittersweet.

Icicle Chimes

Icicles hang like crystal strings,
Beneath their weight, the winter sings.
Each drip a note in a frozen tune,
Echoes of the afternoon.

Sunlight dances on the glass,
Transforming moments as they pass.
Tiny bells of ice so clear,
Resound with every whisper near.

Nature's symphony awake,
In the chill where silence breaks.
Harmonies of frost and air,
Crafted with exquisite care.

Every shimmer, every gleam,
A fragment of a shared dream.
Listen close, embrace the sound,
In icicle chimes, joy is found.

As shadows lengthen, dusk will fall,
Echoes linger, softly call.
In crystal tones, our hearts align,
With winter's breath in pure design.

Twilight in a Frosted Glade

In twilight's hush, the world aglow,
A frosted glade begins to slow.
Soft whispers woven through the trees,
Carried gently on the breeze.

Cold hues blend with fading light,
Turning day into tranquil night.
Footsteps muffled, snowflakes fall,
Blanketing the earth, a peaceful thrall.

The silver moon begins to rise,
A watchful eye in velvet skies.
Stars emerge, a shimmering quilt,
Over a realm that dreams have built.

Frosted branches gently sway,
In this calm, we find our way.
Time stands still, as shadows play,
In twilight's grace, we drift away.

A moment held, beauty unfolds,
In nature's breath, our story told.
Underneath the sky's embrace,
We find our peace, a sacred space.

A Symphony of Snowdrifts

Gentle whispers touch the ground,
Blanketing the quiet town.
Each flake a note, a soft refrain,
Together they sing, a winter's gain.

In the hush of white, time stands still,
Nature's canvas, pure and chill.
Footprints fade in the evening light,
As stars emerge, twinkling bright.

Trees adorned in icy lace,
Silence wraps this sacred space.
A symphony of peace unfolds,
In winter's grasp, a tale retold.

Beneath the moon, shadows play,
Glowing softly, leading the way.
Each drift a story waiting to be,
Told by the night, wild and free.

With every breath, the world inhales,
Magic mingles in frosty trails.
And as dawn breaks, hues ignite,
The symphony wakes, bathed in light.

Frosty Footfalls

In the early morning hush,
Footsteps crunch in chilly rush.
Each imprint tells a silent tale,
Of wanderers roaming the snow-white veil.

The air is crisp, a bite so sweet,
Nature's breath beneath our feet.
Trees wear coats of glistening white,
Guiding us into the soft twilight.

With every step, the world does pause,
The magic born from winter's cause.
Frosty breath mingles in the air,
A season's charm, beyond compare.

Through frozen paths, the heart will roam,
In this wonderland, we find our home.
Each frosty footfall, a note in time,
A melody of peace in winter's rhyme.

As dusk descends, the stars appear,
Whispering dreams, the world draws near.
In the quiet, a warmth enfolds,
Frosty footfalls, a story told.

The Last Leaf of Autumn

A single leaf clings to its bough,
Whispers of change are felt somehow.
Gold and crimson in fading light,
A dance with the breeze, a fleeting sight.

The trees stand barren, stripped and bare,
As winter's chill whispers in the air.
But this lone leaf, with courage bold,
Holds on tightly, a story untold.

Underneath skies of grey and blue,
Memories linger of warmth we knew.
Moments of laughter, bright and alive,
In the heart of this leaf, they still thrive.

As the winds grow stronger, it starts to sway,
The last leaf knows it cannot stay.
Embracing the change, it bids adieu,
Knowing spring's promise shall soon renew.

With a final flutter, it takes to flight,
A journey beyond the autumn night.
Falling softly, it joins the ground,
In nature's cycle, profound and sound.

Nighthawks and Snow Shadows

Under the blanket of starlit skies,
Nighthawks glide with silent cries.
Shadows dance on the snow below,
In the calm of night, their wings aglow.

Moonlight washes the world in grace,
Casting magic in this quiet place.
Each flap of wings, a whisper of night,
Painting the dark with ethereal light.

The chill of air, a frosty kiss,
Wrapped in stillness, a moment of bliss.
In the distance, soft hoots call,
Echoing secrets, enthralling all.

Footsteps vanish, lost in time,
As dreams take flight, unchained, sublime.
In this realm where shadows play,
Nighthawks lead us, come what may.

As dawn nears, the night withdraws,
Hushed now, nature takes a pause.
But every memory of flight remains,
In the whispers of wind, in soft refrains.

Glacial Harmonies

In frozen realms where silence sings,
Icicles dance on whispered wings.
Each crystal note a story told,
Of winter's grip, both fierce and bold.

Majestic peaks with snow adorned,
In twilight hours they stand, unscorned.
A symphony of light and shade,
Where nature's beauty shan't ever fade.

The air is crisp, the world aglow,
As soft flakes fall, a silent show.
Beneath the stars, the landscape sleeps,
In dreams of frost, the heart still keeps.

Echoing through the icy night,
Glacial rhythms, pure delight.
Harmony in every breath,
In winter's song, we find no death.

So let us linger, hand in hand,
In this serene, enchanted land.
For in the glacial gleam we find,
A peaceful heart, a tranquil mind.

Whispering Winds of December

The winds arrive with secrets low,
A chill that speaks of time's soft flow.
Through barren trees they weave and sway,
A gentle tune of winter's play.

They curl around the frosty eves,
Calling out to the hearths and leaves.
Each gust a herald of the night,
Wrapped in whispers, soft and light.

Underneath the starry gaze,
Echoes of the past amaze.
Every breath a fleeting dream,
In December's grasp, we silently gleam.

The world is hushed, each sound is rare,
In the stillness, we find despair.
Yet in the chill, a warmth remains,
A hope that in the heart, sustains.

So let the whispers fill the air,
With tales of solace, love, and care.
In every gust, a promise flows,
Through winter's chill, our spirit grows.

The Quietude of Frost

In morning's light, a blanket white,
Cloaks the earth in pure delight.
Each frost-kissed blade, a diamond's glow,
In quietude, the world moves slow.

Silence reigns in the frozen haze,
As nature pauses, lost in gaze.
Breath of winter, cool and clear,
Inviting peace, so near, so dear.

Trees stand still, their branches bare,
Wrapped in stillness, light as air.
The moments drift like drifting snow,
In quietude, our spirits grow.

A world transformed, serene and bright,
In the crisp calm of fading light.
Frost's embrace, a gentle sigh,
A fleeting touch as time slips by.

Let us wander, hand in hand,
Through the quiet, enchanted land.
In every breath, a frozen thought,
In winter's heart, our dreams are caught.

Shadows in the Snowlight

As dusk descends, the shadows play,
In snowlight's glow, they drift away.
Each flake a whisper, soft and clear,
In twilight hours, all loss draws near.

Footprints left in soft white trails,
A story spun where silence hails.
Beneath the moon, the shadows weave,
In winter's grasp, they gently leave.

The cool embrace of night's descent,
A tranquil heart that time has lent.
In every corner, mystery stirs,
As night unfolds, the frosty purrs.

The world transformed, a silver blank,
In shadows deep, our thoughts we thank.
For winter's grip, while cold and tight,
Holds hidden beauty in the night.

So let us wander, lost in dreams,
In shadows where the moonlight gleams.
Beneath the stars, our hopes ignite,
In the gently falling snowlight.

Crystal Lullaby

In the silence, dreams take flight,
Crystal whispers of the night.
Softly, shadows dance and play,
In a tranquil, shimmering sway.

Moonlight bathes the world in glow,
Gentle breezes start to flow.
Lullabies in silver threads,
Cradle hearts in silky beds.

Stars above in twinkling grace,
Wrap the night in warm embrace.
Each note sings of peace and calm,
In this sphere, a healing balm.

Crystal flutes in distant lands,
Swaying gently, dreamy strands.
Harmony from night's own chest,
In this lullaby, we rest.

Whispers soft as morning dew,
Dreamers find their paths anew.
In the stillness, time stands still,
Crystal lullabies gently thrill.

Hushed Melodies of the Cold

On frost-kissed nights, the world is still,
Hushed melodies, a tranquil thrill.
Gentle whispers in the air,
Nature's song, a pure affair.

Snowflakes fall in soft ballet,
Dancing lightly on their way.
Every flake, a note so rare,
Played in silence, everywhere.

Crystal trees, adorned in white,
Reflect the moon's soft, silver light.
Harmonies of winter's breath,
A serenade, a dance with death.

Chilling winds, they sweep the land,
Each note perfectly unplanned.
In the cold, the world does pause,
Hushed melodies, without because.

Warmth found in the cold's embrace,
A tender moment, time and space.
Through the chill, a heart does beat,
In this quiet, life is sweet.

Frosted Fables

In whispered tales of icy dreams,
Frosted fables, nothing seems.
Glimmering paths through silver trees,
Woven gently by winter's breeze.

Stories wrapped in snowflakes' glow,
Tales of warmth in cold winds blow.
Creatures stir from slumber deep,
In frosted woods, old secrets keep.

Each branch tells a story true,
Of sunlit days and skies so blue.
In every whisper, echoes ring,
Fables of love, the heart does sing.

With every sigh, the night unfolds,
Frosted fables, memories told.
In layers thick, the past is spun,
Embracing shadows, losing none.

From winter's grasp, the tales will flow,
As seasons change and rivers glow.
Frosted fables never die,
In hearts and minds, they always sigh.

Echoes of a Frozen Dawn

At dawn's first light, the world awakes,
Echoes linger, silence breaks.
Frosty fields, a gleaming sight,
Whispers of the coming light.

Golden rays, cut through the chill,
In frozen air, time seems to stand still.
Birds take flight, a joyous sound,
In this moment, peace is found.

Nature stirs, a gentle yawn,
Echoes wane as day is drawn.
Icicles drip in soft refrain,
Releasing whispers of the rain.

Morning warms the icy ground,
Hushed reactions, all around.
In the light, shadows dance fast,
Echoes of the night now past.

Colors bloom, the world transforms,
Frozen dawn, a journey forms.
In every echo, life does swell,
A story told in morning's spell.

A Dance of Falling Snow

Gentle flakes descend with grace,
A soft blanket on the ground.
In silvery silence, they embrace,
The world in beauty, all around.

Whirling whispers in the night,
Each flake tells a tale anew.
Underneath the pale moonlight,
Dreams and wishes float like dew.

Children laugh and dance with glee,
Making angels in the white.
Nature's canvas, wild and free,
A sparkling, frosty delight.

Footprints crunch in twilight's glow,
Marking paths where hearts have tread.
A magical, serene tableau,
As winter wraps the earth in red.

So let us cherish what we see,
A fleeting beauty, pure and bright.
In every flake, a memory,
A dance of falling snow, our light.

Whispers of the Wind

The wind carries a soft sigh,
Through branches swaying, ever near.
It rustles leaves and lifts them high,
A language only we can hear.

In secret, it tells tales of old,
Of mountains, valleys, skies so vast.
With melodies both shy and bold,
It weaves the future with the past.

Caressing fields of ripened grain,
It dances lightly, swift and free.
A soothing balm, a sweet refrain,
The wind, it whispers, "Come and see."

A gentle breeze, a force so strong,
It lifts our spirits, stirs our dreams.
It carries us where we belong,
To places danced in silver beams.

So close your eyes and feel its flow,
Let every heartbeat drift away.
In whispers of the wind, we know,
A journey waits in every sway.

The Cold Caress

A chill wraps softly round my face,
A shiver trailing down my spine.
The cold caress, a crisp embrace,
A winter's breath, both pure and fine.

Frosted air like whispered sighs,
Kisses cheeks with tender grace.
Underneath the starry skies,
I feel the night's soft, cold embrace.

Each crystal flake, a fleeting kiss,
Lands upon my eager skin.
In this icy world, there's bliss,
A quiet peace that lies within.

As trees stand tall with branches bare,
The world is still, serene, and bright.
I close my eyes; I feel the air,
The cold caress, a pure delight.

So let me linger in this chill,
In icy wonders, heart laid bare.
The cold caress, a soothing thrill,
An invitation to breathe in air.

Echoes in the Crystal

In the heart of winter's dream,
Echoes whisper through the trees.
A world transformed by moonlight's beam,
Where silence drifts upon the breeze.

Crystal shards of light surround,
Glistening in the frosty air.
Every sound, a magic sound,
In this realm, without a care.

Footsteps fall on snowy ground,
The crunch a rhythm sweetly played.
In every echo, peace is found,
A tranquil song, serene, delayed.

Memories linger in each breath,
Captured in the frosted haze.
The echoes dance with life and death,
In harmony, they weave their praise.

So close your eyes and hear the call,
In this crystalline, endless night.
Echoes in the dark enthrall,
Their whispers guide us to the light.

The Brush of Winter's Hand

Whispers of snowflakes dance in air,
Each flake a promise, crisp and rare.
Branches groan beneath a winter shroud,
Silent sighs from the earth, so loud.

Winter's breath paints the world in white,
Stars blink softly in the quiet night.
Frost-kissed whispers wrap the trees,
In this frozen tapestry, time seems to freeze.

The rivers sleep under ice so thin,
Nature's slumber, a gentle skin.
Footsteps muffled by the weight of snow,
In winter's embrace, we come and we go.

Crisp air carries echoes of cheer,
Gathered warmth, friends drawing near.
Laughter mingles with the chill of night,
In the heart of winter, everything feels right.

With each passing day, the light returns,
But for the frost, our spirit yearns.
A season's grace, a time to admire,
Under winter's brush, we build the fire.

A Song of Frosted Pines

Among the pines, a melody flows,
Breezes carrying tales of snow.
Each needle glimmers under a lace,
Nature sings in this frozen space.

The chilly gusts hum a soft tune,
Under the watch of a pale winter moon.
Branches sway, whisper secrets untold,
In frosted realms where wonders unfold.

The forest breathes in quiet peace,
Winter's quilt brings a sweet release.
Footsteps follow the path of dreams,
In the heart of the woods, nothing is as it seems.

Squirrels dart through a frosty haze,
Juvenile chimes in the winter maze.
Life persists in the depths of cold,
A resilient song waiting to be told.

Underneath the blanket, creatures nest,
Cocooned in warmth, a secret rest.
Frosted pines sing their ancient tale,
In nature's embrace, we shall prevail.

Light of the Shortest Day

Golden hues dance in fleeting light,
Nature fades to the cool of night.
Moments linger, then swiftly fly,
As shadows deepen beneath the sky.

The hush of dusk wraps the land,
Time slips gently through our hand.
Golden whispers fade away,
Embracing all in the shortest day.

Crisp edges where daylight wanes,
Echoing silence, the heart refrains.
Twilight glimmers on the frozen brook,
In every shadow, a story's nook.

The lanterns flicker, fires aglow,
Warmth spills out in the evening's flow.
Gathered close, we share our dreams,
Pondering stars and moonlight beams.

In a world woven of shadow and light,
We forge our hopes, igniting the night.
The cycle turns, the darkness sways,
Embracing the magic of winter's ways.

The Waking Dream of Ice

Beneath the surface, a world lies still,
Captured whispers on the icy hill.
Frozen moments in a crystal trance,
Nature holds her breath; we dare to dance.

The crackle of frost breaks the heavy dawn,
In this waking dream, we linger on.
Reflections shimmer on the frozen stream,
Entwined in visions of a winter dream.

Glistening wonders in a soft embrace,
Every snowflake finds its place.
The world transformed by winter's kiss,
A tranquil hush that breathes like bliss.

Branches creak beneath the weight of time,
Soft echoes in a world so sublime.
Lingering shadows stretch and gleam,
In the heart of winter, we find our dream.

As sunlight breaks, the ice will part,
Yet in its stillness, we find our heart.
In fleeting moments, beauty we chase,
In the waking dream, we embrace the grace.

Winter's Veil

Snow blankets the silent ground,
Whispers of frost in the air abound.
Barren trees reach for the pale sky,
While stars begin to softly sigh.

Crisp nights wrap in silver thread,
As moonlight dances on dreams unsaid.
The world holds its breath, calm and still,
Embraced by winter's gentle chill.

Footprints trace stories on pure white,
In the hush, shadows become light.
Nature's hush brings peace anew,
In the heart of winter, hope breaks through.

Time lingers here in flurries whirled,
Where firelight glimmers, warmth unfurled.
Each breath a cloud, a fleeting kiss,
In winter's veil, we find our bliss.

The Frosted Pen

A pen in hand, dipped in frost,
Ink spills tales of dreams embossed.
Words like snowflakes drift and dance,
Weaving stories in a trance.

Each letter crisp, a winter's breath,
Carving shadows, faint as death.
Thoughts crystallize, twinkling bright,
In this quiet, the ink feels right.

Pages bloom like icy blooms,
Whispers echo in empty rooms.
Silent thoughts on paper spread,
In the chill, where muses tread.

The world outside, a snowy blur,
Yet inside, silence starts to stir.
With every stroke, the magic flows,
Through winter's chill, creativity grows.

Icebound Reverberations

Echoes of a world encased,
In a blanket of ice, gently paced.
Nature's whispers in frozen tones,
Harmonies lost in chilling moans.

Crystal sirens call from the trees,
Melodies carried by the cold breeze.
Each note a shard of winter's song,
In the stillness, we all belong.

Footsteps crunch on the frozen ground,
In the quiet, new rhythms are found.
The heartbeat of winter hums along,
In an icebound world, we hear its song.

Reflections shimmer on icy streams,
Where sunlight dances in frosty gleams.
Each ripple a tale of seasons past,
Echoes of winter, forever cast.

The Icicle's Tale

An icicle hangs, a dagger of light,
Tales of winter woven tight.
Dripping secrets from skies above,
It clings to the edge, a whisper of love.

In crystalline form, it catches the sun,
Reflecting stories of battles won.
Each melt a drop, a fleeting goodbye,
As time flows gently, the edges dry.

Through storms and winds, it stands so tall,
A sentinel held by winter's call.
With every thaw, a history shared,
In the heart of the cold, it bravely dared.

As spring edges close, it starts to fade,
Its beauty a memory, a legacy made.
From frozen moments, life will prevail,
In the end, we remember the icicle's tale.

The Frosted Heart

In winter's grip, a heart does freeze,
With every breath, a quiet peace.
Amidst the cold, the warmth may spark,
As love ignites within the dark.

The frost may bite, but spirits soar,
Through icy nights, we long for more.
A tender touch, a fleeting glance,
In frost's embrace, we find romance.

Beneath the stars, the dreams take flight,
While silver clouds cloak the moonlight.
In whispered tones, our secrets flow,
As shadows dance in the afterglow.

The chill may linger, yet we'll stay,
With hopeful hearts that guide our way.
For though the world turns cold and grey,
Our love will bloom, come what may.

So take my hand, let's brave the cold,
With every story yet untold.
Through frost and fire, our journey starts,
With courage held in a frosted heart.

Wind's Winter Quatrain

The wind sweeps in with icy breath,
Caressing fields that sleep with death.
It twirls the snowflakes through the night,
Transforming earth in purest white.

Trees bow low to the howling sound,
While whispers echo all around.
In nature's dance, we find our peace,
As winter's grip begins to cease.

The world is hushed, in soft arrays,
A blanket warm, where quiet plays.
With every gust, new paths unfold,
In winter's heart, pure stories told.

Together, let us face the chill,
Embrace the cold, then dare to thrill.
For in the winds, our hearts align,
In winter's touch, your hand in mine.

A Whisper of Snowflakes

Gently they fall, the snowflakes dance,
In silent grace, they take their chance.
A whisper soft as dreams at night,
Cloaking the world in softest white.

Each flake unique, a fleeting art,
Brings joy and peace to every heart.
They twirl and spin in frosty air,
An elegant waltz without a care.

Their magic weaves a tale anew,
A shrouded world in sparkling view.
In winter's hush, we find delight,
As snowflakes drift from day to night.

The beauty lies in moments shared,
In laughter bright, in hearts laid bare.
With every flake, a story starts,
A whispered dream that warms our hearts.

So let us dance in winter's glow,
And bask in all the love we know.
With every whisper, snowflakes sound,
A symphony of joy profound.

Chill of the Whispering Wind

The wind whispers low, a frosty sigh,
As shadows stretch beneath the sky.
A chill that rides on silence bold,
Wraps all the earth in a cloak of cold.

Through barren trees and fields of white,
The whispers weave, a haunting sight.
A lullaby for the wandering soul,
In winter's grasp, we feel it whole.

Each gust reveals a hidden spark,
As frost adorns the silent park.
The air is crisp, the night is deep,
In wind's embrace, we softly weep.

With hearts entwined beneath the stars,
We tread the path, no matter how far.
For in the cold, our spirits rise,
In whispered winds, our love defies.

So let the chill of winter's song,
Wrap us close, where we belong.
In every breath, our truth we send,
A dance of hearts, the winds, our friend.

Winter's Breath on Silent Streets

The world is wrapped in quiet white,
Footsteps lost in soft moonlight.
Whispers glide on the chilling air,
As shadows dance without a care.

Frosty windows, stories untold,
Under blankets, the night grows cold.
The trees are dressed in crystal lace,
Time slows down in this sacred space.

Dim lamplight spills on cobblestone,
Echoes linger, a haunting moan.
Stillness breathes through every lane,
In winter's grasp, there's beauty and pain.

Glistening paths, where dreams unfold,
Each breath gives life to stories bold.
In the silence, secrets unfold,
Winter's breath, a tale retold.

Carved in frost, the night's soft sigh,
Underneath the vast, starry sky,
Every moment holds its weight,
As winter whispers of love and fate.

Shimmering Hush of the Frost

Glistening crystals on frosted trees,
They shimmer gently in the breeze.
A quiet hush blankets the ground,
Nature sleeps without a sound.

Silver glimmers on icy streams,
Reflections dance like whispered dreams.
Stars twinkle in the midnight blue,
While frosty air enchants the view.

Beneath the moon, a world aglow,
In winter's charm, the cold winds blow.
Softly, shadows weave and play,
As night embraces the drifting gray.

Chill of air, sweet breath of frost,
In peaceful stillness, nothing's lost.
Every flake, a fleeting dance,
In winter's realm, life takes a chance.

With dawn's light, the world awakes,
A shimmering coat that beauty makes.
In every glint, a promise lies,
In winter's hush, the heart complies.

Twilight's Shroud of White

A blanket woven from the dusk,
White shrouds cover, a cold husk.
Twilight paints the land serene,
In silence where the world has been.

Whispers linger on branches bare,
As frost embraces the wintry air.
Colors fade as stars emerge,
In twilight's grip, shadows surge.

The horizon blushes in deep gray,
While night unfolds its soft ballet.
Magic drifts in the dimming light,
As winter steals the day from sight.

On this canvas, stars ignite,
Guiding dreams into the night.
Twilight wraps with gentle grace,
In winter's hold, we find our place.

Beneath the moon, the chill takes hold,
Each breath is mist, a story told.
In twilight's embrace, we find delight,
Wrapped in winter's soft white shroud, so bright.

Dance of the Ice Crystals

In the quiet of a winter's night,
Ice crystals twirl in silver light.
They freeze in moments, bold and fast,
A fleeting beauty, bound to pass.

Twinkle, twinkle, crystal fair,
Spinning gently in the air.
Whirl and glide, a graceful show,
In the frosty winds that blow.

The moonlight spills on frozen streams,
Where time is still, and nothing's as it seems.
Nature's dancers, a silent parade,
In the heart of winter, memories are made.

Every flake, a unique design,
A whispered story, a frozen line.
They gather softly, in playful peals,
Wearing the night like sparkling shields.

Dance on, crystals, in the chill so deep,
Awaken dreams from their winter sleep.
Together we watch, in silent delight,
As ice crystals waltz through the quiet night.

Night's Frosted Waltz

Under the silver moonlight glow,
Whispers of winter, soft and slow.
Dancing shadows in the night,
Frosty breath in pure delight.

Bare trees adorned with icy lace,
A silent world, a frozen grace.
Stars twinkle in the cold expanse,
Nature's breath, a quiet dance.

Footsteps crunch on fallen snow,
Echoes of winter's tender flow.
In the stillness, hearts entwine,
Lost in this enchanted time.

Glistening gems on branches high,
A tapestry beneath the sky.
The night deepens, dreams unfold,
In frosted waltz, a story told.

As dawn approaches, shadows fade,
But in the heart, the dance won't jade.
For every twirl, each quiet sigh,
Lives on where the memories lie.

Crystal Cascades

Waterfalls of frozen dreams,
Gentle glimmers, silver streams.
Softly flows the crystal tide,
In nature's arms, we softly bide.

Icicles hang like fragile glass,
Captured moments destined to pass.
Each drop falls with a shimmering kiss,
A fleeting world, a perfect bliss.

Whispers of cold, a fleeting breeze,
Among the branches sway the trees.
In the echoes, laughter rings,
As winter's grip softly clings.

Beneath the ice, life stirs anew,
Hidden wonders in frosty blue.
Time flows on, as seasons blend,
In nature's symphony, we mend.

When the thaw comes, and rivers run,
The memories linger, never done.
In crystal cascades, dreams reside,
A dance of seasons, side by side.

The Winter's Heartbeat

Heartbeat of winter, pure and clear,
A gentle rhythm, drawing near.
With every step, the world whispers low,
In this blanket of peaceful snow.

Moonlit paths on a starry night,
Tracks of dreams in purest light.
In the stillness, stories await,
Of love and time, of paths and fate.

Frosty breath and murmuring streams,
In the quiet, we weave our dreams.
A comforting silence, soft and deep,
In winter's embrace, we softly keep.

Branches sway to the winter's tune,
Under the watch of a silver moon.
Each heartbeat echoes, strong and true,
In this moment, just me and you.

As seasons shift and warm light glows,
The heartbeat of winter still flows.
A memory held in each tear and laugh,
In the winter's pulse, our hearts find their path.

Memories of Ice and Fire

Once upon a winter's night,
Fires warmed with flickering light.
Chasing shadows, tales were spun,
Of ice and fire, two worlds as one.

Frozen lakes beneath the stars,
Dancing flames, their warmth ours.
In laughter's glow, we shared our dreams,
In every spark, hope brightly beams.

The crisp air crisp, a chilling bite,
Yet in our hearts, a burning light.
Together we forged our stories bright,
From memories carved, both cold and bright.

As seasons change, the embers fade,
But in our souls, the warmth we've laid.
In every snowflake, a tale of yore,
In every flame, love's endless shore.

So here we stand, both fire and frost,
In every moment, not a thing lost.
For memories of ice and fire,
In our hearts, will never tire.

Frosted Whispers

In the quiet of the night,
Snowflakes fall like whispers,
Softly blanketing the ground,
A lullaby that shimmers.

Branches wear their frosted cloaks,
Glistening under moonlit grace,
Each breath a cloud of dreams,
In this enchanted space.

Footprints lead to nowhere,
As silence wraps around,
Nature holds its breath close,
In this magic found.

Stars twinkle in the black sky,
Their distant light a guide,
While the world, in stillness, waits,
For warmth, which soon will glide.

Frosty whispers fill the air,
A symphony so sweet,
As winter's hand caresses,
Every heart, every beat.

Silent Echoes of Snow

Silent echoes fill the air,
As snowflakes dance and sway,
Their gentle touch a promise,
To turn night into day.

Beneath the vaulted starry dome,
The world feels calm and bright,
Whispers of the frozen breath,
Preserve the magic of night.

Moonbeams weave a silky thread,
Through branches bathed in white,
Every step a fleeting sound,
Echoing pure delight.

The chill wraps tight around my skin,
Yet warmth blooms in my heart,
For in this winter's splendor,
We shall never part.

Silent echoes, timeless tunes,
In scenes of purest grace,
Snowfall cradles memories,
In this sacred space.

Chilling Serenade

A chilling serenade, so sweet,
The winds begin to play,
Frosty notes upon the air,
As night eclipses day.

Icicles hang like crystal dreams,
Each note a silver chime,
Nature sings its winter song,
In perfect, frozen rhyme.

Beneath the blanket of fresh snow,
Soft whispers intertwine,
Melodies of the silent night,
In rhythms so divine.

Stars are the audience tonight,
As they watch the world below,
Captivated by the beauty,
In the gentle, falling snow.

A chilling serenade, it flows,
Through valleys deep and wide,
Inviting every heart to feel,
This winter's magic tide.

The Breath of Ice

The breath of ice whispers low,
As night begins to fall,
Each frosty breath a secret shared,
In the stillness of it all.

Glimmers dance upon the lake,
Reflecting stars above,
Nature's art, a masterpiece,
A canvas filled with love.

Through shivering pines, the breezes roam,
Carrying tales of old,
Of ancient nights where dreams took flight,
In the cold, dark and bold.

Frozen stories linger on,
In the tapestry of night,
Weaving warmth into the chill,
In the shadows of soft light.

The breath of ice surrounds us here,
Guarding wishes untold,
In winter's grasp, we find our peace,
In the whispers of the cold.

Frosted Questions Unanswered

What lies beneath the frost's cold gaze?
Are dreams encased in crystal haze?
Whispers dance on winter's breath,
In silence deep, we ponder death.

Do memories freeze in icy frames?
Or melt away like fleeting flames?
Each question hangs like misty air,
Inbound within the chill's despair.

What tales lie trapped in frozen streams?
Are they mere echoes of lost dreams?
Beneath the layers, secrets hide,
Waiting for warmth to turn the tide.

When spring emerges, will they break?
Or linger longer, frail and fake?
In the heart of winter's vast white,
Questions sparkle in the night.

The answers wait, elusive, shy,
Like snowflakes drifting from the sky.
Frosted moments, quiet, dear,
Unanswered, yet we hold them near.

The Boundless Blue of Winter Sky

Infinite canvas stretched so wide,
Beneath it, quiet landscapes bide.
Each cloud a whisper, soft and slow,
Cocooned in an ethereal glow.

The sun, a gem, shines bright and clear,
Its warmth a promise held so dear.
Yet shadows linger, long and lean,
In the dance of light, a silver sheen.

Here, peace reigns in frosted hue,
As nature dons its cloak of blue.
Each breath a puff, a fleeting sigh,
In harmony with the vast, wide sky.

The trees stand tall, their branches bare,
Entranced in winter's delicate stare.
Birds sing softly, tunes of the cold,
Stories of warmth in silence told.

With each moment, time does stand,
In this cold realm, so beautifully planned.
The boundless blue, a calming sea,
Where winter's heart dances wild and free.

Prism of the Subdued Sun

The sun descends, a muted glow,
Casting shadows soft and low.
Through branches bare, its light does weave,
In tones of gold that softly leave.

A prism forming on the ground,
Where scattered light is found around.
Each ray a thread, a gentle tease,
Connecting moments, hearts at ease.

Colors whisper in twilight's air,
In every shade, a fleeting prayer.
The day surrenders, night takes flight,
In quiet grace, the world ignites.

With every flicker, shadows gleam,
Painting edges, where dreams seem.
The subdued sun, a quiet guide,
Walking with us, side by side.

In this moment, life feels whole,
As light wraps softly 'round the soul.
A prism holding time's embrace,
In the fading glow, a sacred space.

Whirlwinds of Snowflakes

In the hush of winter's breath,
Whirlwinds dance, embracing depth.
Each snowflake falls, a fleeting dream,
In the air, they swirl and gleam.

Hearts entwined in the flurry's grace,
Tracing patterns, a soft embrace.
With every gust, they spin and rise,
Underneath the grayish skies.

A tempest wild of white and chill,
Whispers secrets against the will.
Frosty laughter fills the night,
As snowflakes twirl, a pure delight.

Here, time pauses in the storm,
Nature's dance, a lovely form.
In the whirlwind, spirits bloom,
As winter's magic fills the room.

With each flake, a wish flies high,
Glistening beneath the silver sky.
Whirlwinds of snowflakes, a ballet true,
In a world of white, in magic anew.

Winter's Embrace

The world is blanketed in white,
Glistening under pale moonlight.
Trees wear coats of crystal cool,
Nature's beauty, a winter jewel.

Chill winds whisper through the air,
With joy, the snowflakes dance and share.
Footprints trace a solitary path,
In this serene, frozen bath.

The night is silent, stars abound,
In this quiet, magic is found.
A world transformed in night's embrace,
Softly sleeping, a tranquil place.

As firelight flickers, warmth inside,
Dreams unfold in the snowy tide.
Hearts find peace in winter's grace,
Nature's love in every space.

Wrapped in layers, cozy and warm,
Winter's charm holds us in swarm.
In each flake, a story's spun,
Winter's embrace, our hearts are won.

Frosted Dreams

Underneath the night so clear,
Stars above, I hold you near.
Frosted dreams begin to soar,
Whispers of what lies in store.

Each snowflake tells a tale untold,
Of winter nights both nice and cold.
In the silence, hearts entwine,
Crafting dreams that brightly shine.

The moonlight casts a silver glow,
Upon the fields of purest snow.
Nature's palette, stark and bright,
Painting visions in the night.

With every breath, the cold arrives,
In this stillness, the spirit thrives.
Frosted windows, candles glow,
Filling hearts with warmth, aglow.

In the quiet, hopes take flight,
Chasing shadows into light.
Frosted dreams guide us through,
Winter whispers, soft and true.

The Silent Nightingale

In a garden cloaked in frost,
The nightingale sings, no sound lost.
Beneath the stars, it finds its voice,
In winter's hush, we still rejoice.

With every note, the world feels new,
Echoes dance, the sky turns blue.
A melody through branches weaves,
Calling warmth, as winter grieves.

The moonlit night, a canvas vast,
Where time slows down, shadows cast.
In this tranquility profound,
The silent song of joy is found.

As dawn breaks, the notes still linger,
Nature's whispers touch each finger.
The nightingale in silence flies,
Sweet lullabies beneath the skies.

Together dreams and hopes entwined,
In the quiet, peace we find.
The silent nightingale, it seems,
Carries forth our winter dreams.

Snowfall's Rhapsody

Snowflakes falling, soft ballet,
Whirling gently, here to stay.
A curtain white, the earth to grace,
Whispers of winter's tight embrace.

Children laughing, spirits bright,
Building castles, pure delight.
Snowball fights in frosty air,
Every moment, free of care.

Nature sings a silent tune,
Underneath the silver moon.
Each flake unique, a fleeting kiss,
In this rhapsody, we find bliss.

The world transformed by winter's hand,
A wonderland, a magic land.
With every flurry, joy bestowed,
In snowfall's dance, our hearts are flowed.

As day fades to a starry night,
Fires crackle, warm and bright.
Embraced in warmth, both soft and snug,
In snow's embrace, we find love's hug.

Solitude of the Snowflakes

In silence they drift, soft and white,
Each flake a whisper, delicate flight.
Blanketing earth in a shroud of peace,
Nature's soft song, a winter's release.

Amidst the chill, a world stands still,
The beauty of cold, embracing the thrill.
Patterns of softness, unique and shy,
Briefly they glisten, before they must die.

Falling from heights, they dance with the air,
Each one's a story, a moment to share.
In the cold embrace, they gather and play,
Lost in their solitude, night turns to day.

Yet in their stillness, a warmth does ignite,
Kindred spirits, in the soft light.
They melt into puddles, dissolve into streams,
Whispers of winter, lost in our dreams.

So here in this moment, let us behold,
The solitude of snowflakes, stories untold.
In their fleeting presence, beauty unveils,
Nature's soft armor, in silence, it trails.

Owls in the Moonlight

In quiet woods where shadows creep,
The owls awake, from their gentle sleep.
With eyes like lanterns, they silently glide,
Guardians of night, where secrets reside.

Under the moon, their feathers blend,
Echoes of wisdom, on they descend.
A soft rustle heard, as they swoop and soar,
Hunters of silence, forever explore.

As night deepens, their calls resound,
A symphony played where dreams abound.
Each hoot tells a tale, of ancient lore,
Of twilight's embrace, that forever more.

Upon tree branches, they perch with grace,
Wisdom etched deep within each face.
They watch the world in the moon's gentle glow,
Guiding lost souls through the night's ebb and flow.

So let us honor these spirits of night,
The owls in the moonlight, a mesmerizing sight.
In their haunting calls, we find our way,
As we wander through night, till the break of day.

Frosted Horizons

Beyond the valleys, a frost sets in,
Painting the dawn with a glimmering skin.
Fields of white stretch, endless and wide,
Whispers of winter, where dreams coincide.

Trees wear coats of shimmering ice,
Reflecting the morning, so bold and nice.
Every branch dances, a crystal array,
As sunlight kisses the frost away.

In this still moment, all seems to gleam,
Nature's own canvas, a painter's dream.
The hush of the world, a serene embrace,
In frosted horizons, we find our place.

Footprints are etched on a sparkling stage,
Every step taken, a story, a page.
As shadows dance softly, the day starts to break,
Waking the slumbering earth from its ache.

So here at the edge of the winter's brow,
We marvel at beauty, oh, here and now.
Frosted horizons, where visions align,
A canvas of wonder, so pure and divine.

A Binary of Snow and Sun

In morning's embrace, both cold and warm,
Snowflakes glisten, nature's charm.
A dance of elements, a vivid display,
Winter meets spring, in an infinite ballet.

Sunlight filters through branches bare,
Creating illusions, pure and rare.
Every flake sparkles, reflecting the light,
A union of worlds, both day and night.

This binary phase, in a fleeting glance,
Harmonious rhythms, a timeless dance.
With every sigh, the landscape transforms,
As snow melts gently, and warmth reforms.

Witness the beauty, the ebb and the flow,
Of snow and sun's grace in a radiant show.
In this brief moment, they hold hands tight,
Creating a magic that fades with the night.

So cherish the balance where contrasts meet,
In the binary of snow and sun, a treat.
For in this embrace, life starts anew,
A symphony of seasons, a breathtaking view.

A Tapestry of Frost and Light

Silvery threads weave through the night,
Dancing softly in the pale moonlight.
Each flake tells a story, pure and bright,
In this frozen world, a wondrous sight.

Glistening branches, jewels on a tree,
Nature's artwork for all to see.
Whispers of winter, wild and free,
A tapestry woven, a symphony.

The stars above twinkle with delight,
Casting dreams on this canvas of white.
Every moment, fleeting as a kite,
Frost and light together ignite.

In silence, the night cradles its grace,
Time stands still in this tranquil space.
We walk in wonder, a gentle pace,
A tapestry of frost, our hearts embrace.

As dawn approaches with gentle hue,
The world awakens, fresh and new.
The tapestry fades but leaves a clue,
Of magic moments, forever true.

The Hearth's Warm Embrace

Crackling embers, a soothing sound,
In this cozy haven, peace is found.
The hearth's warm glow, a circle round,
A refuge from the chill profound.

Gathered close, we share our tales,
As laughter rises, joy prevails.
Through winter's gusts and howling gales,
The hearth endures, its warmth never fails.

A mug of cider, spiced just right,
Bringing comfort on a cold night.
In our hearts, a flame burns bright,
Beneath the stars, all feels so right.

Memories linger, fading light,
Each moment cherished, held so tight.
A family bond woven tight,
In the hearth's embrace, dreams take flight.

As winter wanes and spring draws near,
The fires flicker, but hearts hold dear.
In every echo, in every cheer,
The hearth remains, forever near.

Shadows in the Winter Glow

As daylight wanes, shadows creep,
In winter's glow, the silence deep.
Softly falling, the snow does sweep,
A blanket white, where dreams may sleep.

Flickers of light dance on the floor,
Tales of the past knock on the door.
In the glow of dusk, our spirits soar,
Finding warmth in what we adore.

Footprints linger on frozen ground,
Each step a memory, gently found.
Voices whisper, echoes abound,
In shadows where our hearts are bound.

The fire crackles, the world stands still,
Chilled outside, but in here, a thrill.
With every heartbeat, we bend to will,
New stories waiting, a vast goodwill.

Night unfolds with a silver plume,
In the winter glow, dispelling gloom.
We gather close, like flowers in bloom,
In shadows cast, love finds room.

Whispers of the Frozen Landscape

Vast and quiet, the snow-clad hills,
Nature speaks softly, the heart stills.
Each breath of frost, the air fulfills,
In whispers of beauty, the silence thrills.

Tall pines stand guard, dressed in white,
Frozen moments glimmer with light.
As the world lies wrapped in night,
Whispers of winter create delight.

The brook is hushed, its flow held tight,
Icy fingers clasp, refusing flight.
In the crystal clear, all feels just right,
Nature's canvas, pure and bright.

Footprints marked on the pristine snow,
Trailing stories where few may go.
In the hush, the winds gently blow,
Carrying whispers, soft and slow.

As dawn approaches, the sky ignites,
Colors awaken, banishing nights.
In every shadow, a story fights,
Whispers of the frozen, pure delights.

Milton Keynes UK
Ingram Content Group UK Ltd.
UKHW010231111224
452348UK00011B/685